NARCISSISTIC ABUSE RECOVERY

A Comprehensive Guide to Healing and Thriving After Emotional Manipulation

AUBREY B. MILLS

***Disclaimer:** This book is a work of nonfiction. The information and opinions expressed in this book are those of the author and do not necessarily reflect the views of the publisher.*

TABLE OF CONTENT

INTRODUCTION

Narcissistic abuse is a profoundly damaging form of emotional trauma, one that strips away the very essence of who you are. It is an insidious cycle of manipulation tactics employed by individuals with narcissistic personality disorder or significant narcissistic traits. At its core, narcissistic abuse is the narcissist's exploitation of another person's empathy, compassion, and capacity to love deeply.

While the narcissist may initially present themselves as your soulmate, the perfect partner or friend you've always longed for, this facade eventually crumbles. Beneath the surface lies an individual driven by an excessive need for admiration, an entitled sense of superiority, and a chilling lack of empathy. The narcissist sees you not as a person to cherish but as an object, a source of narcissistic supply to be extracted and controlled through covert and overt forms of abuse.

Emotional manipulation is the narcissist's weapon of choice, wielded with precision to subjugate and erode your sense of self-worth. Love bombing, the idealization phase at the beginning stages, lures you into a simulated reality of being cherished and adored. You are swept off your feet, intoxicated by flattery, future-faking promises, and a whirlwind of intense positive attention. Until, inevitably, the devaluation phase begins.

Suddenly, you find yourself navigating a minefield of subtle put-downs, dismissive body language, blatant lies, financial abuse, and even physical aggression. The narcissist shifts between playing the victim and the abuser, distorting your reality through a tactic known as gaslighting. Doubting your perception of events, your confidence crumbling, you become entrapped in a mental prison of confusion, self-blame, and excruciating cognitive dissonance.

The narcissist's modus operandi is to systematically strip away your independence, self-esteem, and support systems. Employing tactics of isolation, they drive a wedge between you and your loved ones, ensuring your reality exists exclusively within the confines of their dominion. You may find yourself apologizing incessantly, tiptoeing around eggshells, and suppressing your own wants and needs.

The trauma of narcissistic abuse is both psychological and physical, the invisible wounds often more agonizing than visible ones. Complex post-traumatic stress disorder (C-PTSD), depression, anxiety, and other mental health challenges frequently plague survivors, compounded by a deep sense of shame, guilt, and self-loathing instilled by the abuser.

Yet, despite the profoundly damaging effects, there is hope for healing and a path toward reclaiming your sense of self-worth. This book serves as a comprehensive guide, a compassionate companion on your journey from victimhood to survivorship, from merely surviving to thriving.

Within these pages, you will embark on a transformative odyssey, navigating the treacherous terrain of narcissistic abuse recovery. We will begin by shining a light on the narcissist's playbook, examining the disordered personality and manipulation tactics employed. Understanding the psychological profile and motivations behind the abuse is a crucial first step in dismantling the narcissist's power over you.

From there, we will delve into the profound impact of emotional abuse, exploring the psychological, physical, and emotional scars it leaves behind. Recognizing the depth of your trauma is essential for validating your experiences and beginning the healing process.

Once we have laid this foundation, we will chart a course toward freedom and self-reclamation. You will learn strategies for safely extricating yourself from abusive situations, develop tools for managing triggers and complex trauma, and discover the path toward rebuilding your self-worth from the ashes of abuse.

Healing from narcissistic abuse is not a linear journey; it is a spiral, a continuous process of growth, setbacks, and breakthroughs. This book will serve as your trusted guide, illuminating the way forward and equipping you with the insights, exercises, and practices necessary to navigate this cyclical path.

We will explore the art of establishing healthy boundaries, a critical component of self-preservation and protection against future abuse. You will learn to identify the red flags of toxic relationships and cultivate a network of supportive individuals who honor your worth.

Crucially, this book is not merely about surviving; it is about thriving. We will embark on a journey of personal growth and empowerment, rediscovering your passions, pursuing your goals with renewed vigor, and embracing the wisdom that emerges from adversity. You will develop resilience, emotional intelligence, and the ability to extend compassion – to yourself and others who have endured similar hardships.

Throughout these chapters, you will encounter not just insights but actionable exercises, reflections, and practices designed to facilitate your healing journey. From affirmations and self-compassion rituals to trauma-informed mindfulness techniques, you will be equipped with a diverse toolkit to aid in your recovery.

Woven throughout the narrative are the voices and stories of survivors who have walked this path before you – courageous individuals who have not only persevered but flourished in the aftermath of abuse. Their triumphs, hard-won lessons, and enduring hope will serve as beacons, guiding you through the darkest moments and reminding you of the profound resilience within.

Narcissistic abuse recovery is not a destination; it is an ongoing metamorphosis, a shedding of old skins and the emergence of a wiser, more resilient self. This transformation will not happen overnight, nor will it be without its challenges. There will be moments when the pain feels insurmountable, when the path seems shrouded in darkness. Yet, with each step forward, you will find your footing growing surer, your voice growing louder, and your spirit becoming more indomitable.

By the final pages of this book, you will have cultivated a profound understanding of the abuse cycle, a reservoir of self-compassion, and an arsenal of strategies to safeguard your healing. You will have learned to forgive yourself for the past, to live authentically in the present, and to dream boldly about the future.

Most importantly, you will have reclaimed your identity - not as a victim, but as a survivor, a warrior, and an individual worthy of profound respect and unconditional love, starting with the love you have for yourself.

The road ahead will not be easy, but you are not alone. This book is your unwavering companion, a beacon of wisdom and a testament to the human spirit's ability to rise, like a phoenix, from the ashes of even the darkest abuse.

Are you ready to begin your journey? Then let us take the first step, together.

PART 1

UNDERSTANDING

NARCISSISTIC ABUSE

CHAPTER 1

THE NARCISSIST'S PLAYBOOK

To understand the insidious nature of narcissistic abuse, we must first shed light on the psychological profile and disordered thinking that fuel the narcissist's behaviors. While narcissistic personality disorder (NPD) exists on a spectrum, those who exhibit pronounced narcissistic traits tend to operate from a similar playbook - a compendium of manipulation tactics designed to exploit, control, and subjugate their victims.

At the core of narcissistic personality disorder lies a paradoxical dichotomy - an inflated, grandiose sense of self-importance coupled with a profound lack of self-esteem. The narcissist's ego is a delicate construct, a facade precariously maintained through the admiration and difference of others. Beneath this mask lies a deep well of insecurity, emotional dysregulation, and an acute fear of being perceived as ordinary or inadequate.

The narcissist's psyche is governed by a relentless pursuit of narcissistic supply – the attention, praise, and validation that fuels their fragile sense of superiority. People become mere instruments in this quest, objects to be acquired, idealized, and ultimately discarded when they cease to serve the narcissist's needs. Empathy, genuine emotional intimacy, and the ability to view others as fully autonomous human beings are profoundly impaired.

This disordered mindset manifests in a constellation of traits and behaviors that form the narcissist's modus operandi. Let us delve into the central characteristics that define this personality disorder and the tactics employed to ensnare and subjugate victims.

Grandiose Sense of Self-Importance

The narcissist's inflated ego drives an unwavering belief in their own superiority, uniqueness, and entitlement. They perceive themselves as special, exceptional individuals deserving of excessive admiration and preferential treatment. This grandiose sense of self-importance often manifests as arrogant, boastful behavior, a propensity to monopolize conversations, and an insatiable need to be the center of attention.

Preoccupation with Fantasies of Success, Power, and Brilliance

Narcissists are consumed by grandiose fantasies of unlimited success, power, beauty, or intellectual prowess. They harbor an unshakable belief in their destiny for greatness, often exaggerating their accomplishments, talents, and potential. These unrealistic expectations and delusions of grandeur serve to bolster their fragile egos and justify their sense of entitlement.

Lack of Empathy

One of the most defining traits of narcissistic personality disorder is a profound deficit in empathy – the ability to understand and share the feelings of others. Narcissists view the world through a distorted lens of self-absorption, rendering them incapable of truly considering the needs, perspectives, or emotional experiences of those around them.

People become mere objects, instruments to be manipulated for personal gain or sources of narcissistic supply.

Exploitative and Entitled Behavior

Driven by an acute sense of entitlement, narcissists have no qualms about exploiting others for their own benefit. They operate under the assumption that they deserve special treatment, privileges, and unquestioning compliance from those around them. This entitlement often manifests as a willingness to take advantage of others, violate their boundaries, and disregard their rights in pursuit of personal gratification.

Lack of Emotional Intimacy and Depth

True emotional intimacy requires vulnerability, reciprocity, and a genuine interest in understanding the inner worlds of others – capacities that narcissists sorely lack. Relationships with narcissists are often superficial, devoid of the depth and emotional richness that characterize healthy bonds. The narcissist's inability to empathize and their self-absorption create an emotional void, leaving their partners or loved ones feeling profoundly alone and unseen.

Envy and a Begrudging Attitude

Narcissists harbor intense feelings of envy toward those who possess qualities, accomplishments, or traits they perceive as threatening to their own sense of superiority. This envy often breeds resentment, contempt, and a begrudging attitude, as the narcissist seeks to diminish or devalue others to protect their inflated egos. Celebrations of others' successes are often met with disdain, sarcasm, or outright hostility.

Arrogant and Haughty Behaviors and Attitudes

Arrogance and a haughty, dismissive demeanor are common defense mechanisms employed by narcissists to maintain their perceived superiority. They often engage in condescending behaviors, belittling others' opinions, achievements, or perspectives. This arrogance serves as a shield, deflecting any perceived threats to their fragile egos and reinforcing their grandiose self-perceptions.

With an understanding of the core traits that define narcissistic personality disorder, we can now examine the specific tactics and manipulation strategies employed by narcissists to ensnare, exploit, and control their victims.

Love Bombing

The narcissist's playbook often begins with a tactic known as love bombing – a deluge of excessive affection, attention, and idealization designed to overwhelm and ensnare their target. In the initial stages of a relationship, the narcissist will shower their victim with flattery, grand romantic gestures, and promises of an epic, fairytale-like bond.

This intense courtship serves several purposes: it creates a powerful emotional high and sense of connection, making the victim feel special and deeply appreciated. It also establishes a stark contrast with the devaluation and abuse that will inevitably follow, contributing to the trauma bond that keeps victims entrapped. Love bombing sets the stage for the narcissist's manipulation, priming the victim to overlook red flags and cementing the belief that their abuser is truly the perfect partner they've longed for.

Gaslighting

Gaslighting is a form of psychological manipulation that erodes the victim's sense of reality and self-trust. The narcissist systematically distorts facts, denies or minimizes the victim's experiences, and projects their own behaviors and motivations onto their target.

Through gaslighting, the narcissist cultivates an atmosphere of confusion, self-doubt, and cognitive dissonance within their victim. They may blatantly lie, contradict themselves, or rewrite history, leaving the victim questioning their own memories and perceptions. This tactic serves to undermine the victim's confidence, making them more reliant on the narcissist's version of reality and more susceptible to further manipulation.

Silent Treatment and Stonewalling

The silent treatment and stonewalling are powerful tools in the narcissist's arsenal, designed to exert control, punish perceived transgressions, and induce a state of anxiety and desperation within the victim.

By abruptly withdrawing communication, affection, and attention without explanation, the narcissist creates an agonizing void, leaving the victim grasping for crumbs of attention and validation. This tactic reinforces the victim's codependency, forcing them to walk on eggshells and contort themselves to regain the narcissist's approval.

The silent treatment is often deployed in response to any perceived slight or challenge to the narcissist's authority, serving as a means of asserting dominance and instilling fear of abandonment within the victim.

Blame-Shifting and Deflection

Narcissists are masterful at shifting blame and deflecting responsibility for their hurtful behaviors onto their victims. When confronted with the consequences of their actions or the pain they have inflicted, they will deftly maneuver the conversation to implicate the victim as the root cause.

Through blame-shifting, the narcissist absolves themselves of accountability and reinforces the victim's self-doubt. The victim is left questioning their own perceptions, internalizing the narcissist's narrative of events, and ultimately accepting responsibility for the abuse they have endured.

Triangulation and Divide-and-Conquer

Triangulation is a manipulation tactic in which the narcissist fosters competition, comparisons, and division among their victims or those in their social circles. By pitting people against one another, the narcissist sows seeds of jealousy, insecurity, and mistrust, reinforcing their position of power and control.

This tactic is often employed within romantic relationships, where the narcissist may openly flirt with or show favoritism toward others, creating a sense of perceived rivalry and instability. In social circles or families, the narcissist may share confidential information or gossip, driving wedges between relationships and isolating their primary target from potential support systems.

Trauma Bonding and Intermittent Reinforcement

Central to the narcissist's ability to trap their victims in a cycle of abuse is the insidious phenomenon of trauma bonding. This bond forms through a pattern of intermittent reinforcement, where the narcissist alternates between cruelty and kindness, abuse and idealization.

During the idealization phase, the narcissist showers their victim with affection, praise, and promises, triggering a powerful emotional high and reinforcing the victim's attachment. This is swiftly followed by the devaluation phase, where the narcissist unleashes a barrage of criticism, emotional abuse, and mistreatment.

This cyclical pattern creates a potent trauma bond, akin to Stockholm syndrome, where the victim becomes psychologically and emotionally dependent on their abuser. The sporadic reinforcement of kindness and the fear of abandonment make it excruciatingly difficult for the victim to escape the cycle of abuse.

The Narcissistic Abuse Cycle

The narcissist's tactics coalesce into a well-established cycle of abuse, a Machiavellian dance of idealization, devaluation, and discarding that entraps the victim in a perpetual state of confusion, self-doubt, and emotional turmoil.

The cycle begins with the idealization phase, where the narcissist projects an image of perfection, showering their target with excessive adoration, flattery, and future-faking promises. This love bombing creates a powerful emotional high and a deep sense of connection, effectively blindsiding the victim to any potential red flags.

As the narcissist's mask slips, the devaluation phase commences. The victim finds themselves navigating a minefield of manipulation tactics – gaslighting, silent treatment, blame-shifting, and triangulation. The once-idyllic partner transforms into a cruel, demeaning abuser, leaving the victim reeling from cognitive dissonance and struggling to reconcile the stark contrast.

The final stage is the discard phase, where the narcissist abruptly abandons or casts aside their victim, often in favor of a new source of narcissistic supply. This brutal rejection compounds the victim's trauma, leaving them grappling with profound feelings of worthlessness, shame, and self-blame.

Yet, the cycle does not end there. Often, the narcissist will initiate a hoover phase, employing tactics such as love bombing, manipulation, or even threats to reel their victim back into the vortex of abuse. This cyclical pattern of idealization, devaluation, and discarding can repeat endlessly, perpetuating the trauma bond and making it increasingly difficult for the victim to break free.

By understanding the narcissist's playbook - the disordered mindset, manipulation tactics, and cyclical abuse patterns - we can begin to dismantle the power these individuals hold over their victims. Knowledge is the first step in reclaiming our agency, our self-worth, and our freedom from the clutches of narcissistic abuse.

CHAPTER 2

THE IMPACT OF EMOTIONAL ABUSE

The scars of narcissistic abuse run deeper than the eye can perceive. While physical violence leaves visible marks, the invisible wounds inflicted by emotional and psychological trauma can be equally, if not more, agonizing and long-lasting. The impact of this insidious form of abuse permeates every fiber of a survivor's being, affecting their mental, physical, and emotional well-being in profound ways.

To embark on the journey of healing, we must first shed light on the devastation wrought by emotional manipulation. By understanding the multi-faceted effects of narcissistic abuse, we can validate the immense challenges survivors face and appreciate the courage required to overcome them.

Psychological Effects: A Shattered Self-Concept

At the core of narcissistic abuse lies an assault on the victim's sense of self – a systematic erosion of their identity, self-worth, and autonomy. The psychological impact of this trauma can manifest in a myriad of ways, each exacerbating the other in a vicious cycle of self-doubt and anguish.

Low Self-Esteem and Self-Loathing

Constant criticism, belittling, and invalidation are hallmarks of emotional abuse, chipping away at the victim's self-esteem until it lies in tatters. Survivors often internalize the narcissist's dehumanizing narratives, plagued by deep-rooted feelings of inadequacy, worthlessness, and self-loathing. The very essence of who they are becomes distorted through the abuser's lens, leaving them questioning their value, talents, and intrinsic worth.

Anxiety and Hypervigilance

Living in a state of perpetual fear and walking on eggshells is the norm for those entrapped in narcissistic abuse cycles. The unpredictability of the narcissist's behavior, coupled with the ever-present threat of punishment or abandonment, cultivates a constant state of anxiety and hypervigilance within the victim.

Even after escaping the abusive situation, survivors may find themselves plagued by intrusive thoughts, racing hearts, and a persistent sense of dread – remnants of the trauma that have become deeply ingrained in their psyche. This hypervigilance can disrupt daily functioning, strain interpersonal relationships, and foster a pervasive sense of mistrust and insecurity.

Depression and Emotional Dysregulation

The psychological torment inflicted by narcissistic abuse can precipitate profound depressive episodes and emotional dysregulation. Survivors often grapple with feelings of hopelessness, worthlessness, and an inability to experience joy or contentment – the emotional fallout of enduring relentless devaluation, gaslighting, and manipulation.

Emotional dysregulation, or the inability to effectively manage and process emotions, is another common byproduct of abuse. Survivors may find themselves oscillating between extremes – numb detachment, explosive outbursts, or overwhelming surges of sadness, anger, or fear. This dysregulation can impede daily functioning and exacerbate existing mental health struggles.

Complex Post-Traumatic Stress Disorder (C-PTSD)

While Post-Traumatic Stress Disorder (PTSD) is often associated with single-event traumas, such as combat or natural disasters, narcissistic abuse can precipitate a more insidious form known as Complex PTSD (C-PTSD). This condition arises from prolonged, repeated trauma, often inflicted by a trusted individual or caregiver.

Survivors of narcissistic abuse may experience intrusive thoughts, flashbacks, and dissociative episodes that transport them back to the moments of abuse. They may struggle with emotional regulation, develop negative self-perceptions, and exhibit profound difficulties in forming and maintaining healthy relationships – all hallmarks of C-PTSD.

PHYSICAL MANIFESTATIONS: THE BODY KEEPS SCORE

The mind and body are inextricably linked, and the trauma inflicted by emotional abuse can manifest in myriad physical symptoms. These somatic expressions of distress serve as poignant reminders that the scars of narcissistic abuse extend far beyond the psychological realm.

Chronic Stress and Adrenal Fatigue

Living in a constant state of fear, hypervigilance, and emotional turmoil takes a tremendous toll on the body's stress response system. The relentless activation of the fight-or-flight response can lead to adrenal fatigue, a condition characterized by depleted energy reserves, impaired immune function, and a host of other debilitating symptoms.

Chronic stress can also contribute to the development of various health issues, including cardiovascular disease, digestive disorders, and autoimmune conditions – a sobering testament to the inextricable link between emotional trauma and physical well-being.

Chronic Pain and Inflammation

Emotional distress and trauma have a profound impact on the body's inflammatory pathways, often manifesting as chronic pain and inflammation. Survivors of narcissistic abuse may experience unexplained physical ailments such as fibromyalgia, migraines, joint pain, and muscle aches – conditions that can profoundly disrupt daily functioning and quality of life.

The mechanisms behind this mind-body connection are complex, involving intricate interplays between the nervous system, immune function, and the body's stress response. However, the underlying message is clear: the scars of emotional trauma can etch themselves deep into the physical form, creating a feedback loop of suffering that compounds the overall impact of abuse.

Sleep Disturbances and Fatigue

The relentless anxiety, hypervigilance, and intrusive thoughts that plague survivors of narcissistic abuse can wreak havoc on sleep patterns and quality. Insomnia, nightmares, and disrupted circadian rhythms are common experiences, leaving survivors in a perpetual state of exhaustion and fatigue.

Chronic sleep deprivation can exacerbate existing physical and mental health issues, impair cognitive function, and hinder the body's natural healing processes. This vicious cycle of poor sleep and increased distress only serves to amplify the overall burden of the trauma endured.

EMOTIONAL TURMOIL: A KALEIDOSCOPE OF ANGUISH

The emotional impact of narcissistic abuse is perhaps the most insidious and enduring aspect of this trauma. The manipulation tactics employed by abusers leave deep, indelible scars on the emotional landscape of their victims, casting long shadows that can obscure the path to healing and self-reclamation.

Fear and Hypervigilance

Living under the constant threat of punishment, abandonment, or emotional annihilation instills a profound sense of fear and hypervigilance within survivors of narcissistic abuse. Even after escaping the abusive situation, they may find themselves scanning their environments for potential threats, anticipating the next emotional onslaught, and struggling to feel truly safe and grounded.

This persistent state of fear can pervade every aspect of a survivor's life, eroding their sense of security and undermining their ability to form healthy attachments and trust others. Breaking the cycle of hypervigilance is a crucial step in the healing journey, allowing survivors to reclaim a sense of agency and control over their lives.

Shame and Self-Blame

Narcissistic abusers are masterful at deflecting responsibility and shifting blame onto their victims. Through gaslighting, minimization, and projection, they instill a deep sense of shame and self-blame within their targets, convincing them that they are the architects of their own suffering.

This internalized shame can be one of the most pernicious and enduring effects of emotional abuse, corroding self-worth and fostering a belief that the survivor is fundamentally flawed or unworthy of love and respect. Breaking free from this toxic narrative and cultivating self-compassion is a critical step in the healing process, enabling survivors to reclaim their inherent value and shed the burden of undeserved guilt.

Cognitive Dissonance and Confusion

The mind's natural tendency to seek patterns and create meaning can become a double-edged sword in the context of narcissistic abuse. The abuser's manipulation tactics, such as gaslighting and love-bombing, create a state of cognitive dissonance – a profound disconnect between the survivor's experiences and the abuser's distorted narratives.

This dissonance can breed confusion, self-doubt, and a profound erosion of trust in one's own perceptions and reality. Survivors may find themselves questioning their sanity, struggling to reconcile the abuser's Jekyll-and-Hyde behavior, and grappling with the lingering effects of trauma bonding.

Navigating this emotional labyrinth is a formidable challenge, but one that is essential for reclaiming a sense of clarity, self-trust, and grounding in objective reality.

Grief and Loss

Beneath the anguish and turmoil of narcissistic abuse lies a profound sense of grief and loss. Survivors mourn the loss of the idealized partner or relationship they were promised, the loss of their dreams and aspirations, and the loss of the person they once were before the trauma unfolded.

This grief can manifest as sadness, anger, or even a sense of disorientation, as if the ground has shifted beneath their feet. Survivors may find themselves grappling with existential questions, re-evaluating their belief systems, and struggling to make sense of the depth of betrayal they have endured.

Acknowledging and processing this grief is a vital aspect of the healing journey, allowing survivors to honor their losses, integrate their experiences, and pave the way for personal growth and transformation.

THE RIPPLE EFFECT: COLLATERAL DAMAGE

The impact of narcissistic abuse extends far beyond the primary target, casting a long shadow over the survivor's relationships, social circles, and overall quality of life. The collateral damage inflicted by this trauma can manifest in myriad ways, creating ripple effects that reverberate through every aspect of a survivor's existence.

Strained Relationships and Social Isolation

The manipulation tactics employed by narcissistic abusers often involve isolating their victims from support systems, driving wedges between them and their loved ones. This deliberate severing of social ties not only deprives survivors of crucial emotional support but can also breed profound mistrust and difficulty in maintaining healthy relationships.

Even after escaping the abusive situation, survivors may find themselves grappling with the residual effects of this isolation, struggling to rebuild fractured connections or forge new ones. The emotional turmoil and hypervigilance that linger can create barriers to intimacy, fueling a self-perpetuating cycle of loneliness and disconnection.

Disrupted Career and Financial Instability

The insidious nature of narcissistic abuse often extends into the professional realm, with abusers undermining their victims' career ambitions, financial stability, and overall autonomy. Survivors may find themselves grappling with job instability, difficulty maintaining focus or productivity, or even sabotaged educational or professional opportunities.

Financial abuse is another common tactic, where the abuser exerts control over the victim's access to resources, limiting their ability to achieve financial independence or secure a stable future. The ripple effects of these disruptions can be far-reaching, impacting a survivor's long-term financial security, career prospects, and overall quality of life.

Diminished Self-Efficacy and Decision-Making Paralysis

One of the most devastating consequences of narcissistic abuse is the erosion of a survivor's sense of self-efficacy – their belief in their ability to navigate life's challenges and make autonomous decisions. The constant barrage of invalidation, gaslighting, and control tactics employed by the abuser can leave survivors doubting their judgment, second-guessing their choices, and feeling paralyzed in the face of even minor decisions.

This diminished self-efficacy can pervade every aspect of a survivor's life, from personal relationships to professional endeavors, creating a profound sense of disempowerment and hindering their ability to thrive. Reclaiming agency and trust in one's decision-making capabilities is a critical step in the healing journey, allowing survivors to chart their own course and regain a sense of mastery over their lives.

THE ENDURING BATTLE: HEALING FROM NARCISSISTIC ABUSE

As we have explored, the impact of narcissistic abuse is multi-faceted, permeating the psychological, physical, emotional, and social realms of a survivor's life. The journey to healing is not a linear path but a spiraling odyssey, replete with challenges, setbacks, and hard-won victories.

Yet, despite the formidable obstacles, healing is not only possible but a testament to the indomitable resilience of the human spirit. By acknowledging the depth of the trauma endured, validating the myriad ways it manifests, and embracing a holistic approach to recovery, survivors can reclaim their agency, their self-worth, and their right to a fulfilling, joyful existence.

The path ahead is arduous, but each step taken is a defiant act of courage, a declaration of sovereignty over the trauma that once held sway. With determination, self-compassion, and a commitment to personal growth, survivors can emerge from the ashes of narcissistic abuse, not merely as survivors, but as warriors – fortified by their experiences and emboldened to create a life of profound meaning and authenticity.

PART 2

THE IMPACT OF

EMOTIONAL DAMAGE

CHAPTER 3

LEAVING THE ABUSIVE SITUATION

The decision to leave a narcissistic abuser is one of the most courageous and pivotal steps a survivor can take on their journey to healing. It is a leap of faith, a defiant act of self-preservation that shatters the illusion of control carefully cultivated by the abuser. Yet, this momentous choice is often fraught with trepidation, doubt, and overwhelming fear - remnants of the trauma bond and manipulation tactics that have kept the survivor entrapped for so long.

Recognizing the need to leave an abusive situation is a profound act of self-awareness and self-love. It requires seeing through the narcissist's distorted reality and acknowledging the depths of harm inflicted upon one's mind, body, and soul. This awakening can arise gradually, through a series of escalating incidents or revelations, or it can manifest as a sudden, crystallizing moment when the veil of denial is torn asunder.

For some, the realization may come in the form of a visceral reaction to a particularly egregious act of abuse - a physical altercation, a dehumanizing verbal assault, or a betrayal that shatters the last vestiges of trust. For others, it may emerge from the cumulative weight of emotional turmoil, the soul-crushing exhaustion of walking on eggshells, or the dawning recognition that the idealized partner they fell in love with was merely a mirage.

Regardless of the catalyst, the decision to leave is a courageous act of reclamation - a declaration that one's safety, dignity, and well-being are paramount, and that the cycle of abuse must be broken, no matter the cost.

Yet, even as this resolve takes root, the path forward is fraught with obstacles and uncertainties. The narcissist's manipulative tactics have instilled a deep-seated fear of abandonment, financial insecurity, and potential retribution. Doubts may arise, fueled by the gaslighting and cognitive dissonance that have become all too familiar. The trauma bond, forged through cycles of idealization and devaluation, can create a powerful emotional tether, making the prospect of complete severance feel unimaginable.

It is in these moments of wavering that the survivor must draw upon an unwavering reserve of inner strength and self-compassion. They must remind themselves of the depths of suffering endured, the erosion of their identity, and the relentless assault on their autonomy – all consequences of remaining enmeshed in the narcissist's web of control.

SAFETY PLANNING: NAVIGATING THE TREACHEROUS TERRAIN

Leaving a narcissistic abuser is not merely an emotional undertaking; it is a strategic endeavor that requires meticulous planning and a prioritization of one's physical and psychological safety. The narcissist's propensity for retaliation, emotional blackmail, and even escalated violence during periods of perceived abandonment necessitates a comprehensive safety plan.

The first step in this process is creating a support network – a circle of trusted individuals who can offer emotional support, practical assistance, and, if necessary, a safe haven during the transition. This may include family members, close friends, domestic violence advocates, or professionals equipped to guide survivors through the legal and logistical complexities of extracting themselves from an abusive situation.

Fortifying this support system is crucial, as the narcissist will likely employ every manipulation tactic in their arsenal to maintain control, isolate the survivor, and undermine their resolve. Having a robust network of allies who validate the survivor's experiences and reinforce their decision to leave can counteract the gaslighting and self-doubt that so often accompanies this process.

Developing a safety plan also involves securing crucial resources and documents, such as financial records, legal paperwork, and personal identification. The narcissist may attempt to withhold or destroy these materials as a means of exerting control, making it imperative for the survivor to safeguard their access to vital assets and information.

For those in situations where physical violence is a concern, additional safety measures may be necessary, such as establishing a coded communication system with trusted allies, identifying safe houses or shelters, and documenting evidence of abuse for legal purposes.

Throughout this process, it is essential for survivors to prioritize their well-being and seek guidance from domestic violence organizations or law enforcement agencies when necessary. The narcissist's capacity for retaliation and emotional manipulation should never be underestimated, and taking proactive steps to mitigate potential harm is a matter of utmost importance.

ACCESSING SUPPORT RESOURCES

Navigating the complexities of leaving a narcissistic abuser can be an overwhelming and isolating experience. Fortunately, a wealth of resources and support systems exist to guide survivors through this arduous journey, offering invaluable assistance in areas ranging from legal aid to emotional counseling.

Domestic violence organizations and hotlines are often the first line of defense, providing confidential support, safety planning guidance, and connections to local shelters and resources. These organizations are staffed by trained advocates who understand the unique challenges and dynamics of abusive relationships, offering a compassionate ear and practical strategies tailored to each survivor's circumstances.

Legal aid clinics and pro bono attorneys can assist with securing protective orders, navigating divorce or custody proceedings, and addressing financial or housing-related concerns. The legal complexities of extracting oneself from an abusive relationship can be daunting, and having access to knowledgeable professionals can alleviate a significant burden during this transitional period.

For those in need of immediate shelter or emergency housing, domestic violence shelters and safe houses offer a secure haven, providing temporary accommodations, counseling services, and assistance in developing long-term safety plans. These facilities prioritize the privacy and confidentiality of their residents, ensuring that survivors can begin the healing process without fear of retaliation or further abuse.

Support groups and therapy programs specifically tailored to survivors of narcissistic abuse can be invaluable resources for addressing the emotional and psychological fallout of this trauma. These groups provide a safe space for survivors to share their experiences, validate their feelings, and develop coping strategies alongside others who have walked a similar path.

Online communities and forums dedicated to narcissistic abuse recovery can also offer a lifeline, connecting survivors across geographic boundaries and fostering a sense of solidarity in the face of shared struggles. These virtual support networks can be particularly valuable for those in isolated areas or facing obstacles in accessing in-person resources.

Ultimately, the road to freedom from narcissistic abuse is paved with a mosaic of support systems – each offering a unique perspective, specialized expertise, and an unwavering commitment to empowering survivors on their journey to reclaiming their lives.

COPING WITH FEARS, DOUBTS, AND SETBACKS

Even with a robust safety plan and a network of support in place, the process of leaving a narcissistic abuser is inherently fraught with emotional turmoil, self-doubt, and setbacks. The trauma bond forged through cycles of idealization and devaluation can create a powerful gravitational pull, making the prospect of complete severance feel like a monumental feat.

Survivors may find themselves grappling with deep-seated fears of abandonment, financial insecurity, or reprisal from the abuser. These fears, however irrational they may seem from the outside, are deeply rooted in the psychological manipulation and gaslighting tactics employed by the narcissist over an extended period.

It is crucial for survivors to acknowledge and validate these fears without judgment or self-recrimination. The trauma they have endured is profound, and the emotional scars run deep. Seeking support from trusted allies, counselors, or support groups can provide a reassuring counterpoint to the negative self-talk and self-doubt that may arise during this turbulent transition.

Doubts may also creep in, fueled by the narcissist's love-bombing tactics or the romanticized memories of the idealization phase. The survivor may find themselves questioning their decision, minimizing the abuse, or even entertaining the notion of reconciliation – a testament to the insidious nature of the trauma bond.

In these moments of wavering, it is imperative to anchor oneself in the reality of the abuse endured, the erosion of autonomy and self-worth, and the relentless emotional turmoil that characterized the relationship. Journaling, compiling evidence of the abuse, or seeking guidance from a therapist or support group can help reframe the situation and combat the cognitive distortions that so often accompany the healing process.

Setbacks and temporary backsliding are not only common but should be expected on the path to freedom from narcissistic abuse. The narcissist may employ hoovering tactics, using emotional manipulation, love-bombing, or even threats to lure the survivor back into the cycle of abuse.

During these vulnerable moments, it is crucial for survivors to rely on their support network, reinforce their boundaries, and remind themselves of the hard-won progress they have made. Setbacks are not failures; they are opportunities to strengthen resilience, refine coping strategies, and reaffirm one's commitment to healing.

Throughout this arduous journey, self-compassion and patience must be constant companions. Healing from the insidious trauma of narcissistic abuse is a non-linear process, fraught with ebbs and flows, triumphs and stumbles. By extending kindness and understanding to oneself, celebrating small victories, and embracing the support of those who validate their experiences, survivors can navigate these turbulent waters with increasing grace and fortitude.

The path to freedom is rarely a straight line, but each step taken is a defiant act of courage, a testament to the indomitable resilience of the human spirit. With perseverance, self-love, and a steadfast commitment to personal growth, the chains of narcissistic abuse can be broken, and a life of authenticity and fulfillment can be reclaimed.

CHAPTER 4

UNPACKING THE TRAUMA

The arduous journey of leaving a narcissistic abuser is merely the first step on the long road to healing and reclamation. The trauma endured during the cycles of idealization, devaluation, and discard has left indelible scars – wounds that must be tended to with care, compassion, and a deep understanding of the unique psychological impacts of this insidious form of abuse.

As survivors embark on the next phase of their odyssey, they must confront the complex manifestations of their trauma head-on, unpacking the layers of emotional turmoil, cognitive distortions, and physiological dysregulation that have become ingrained in their psyche. This process is not merely a matter of introspection but a holistic exploration of the mind, body, and spirit – a journey that requires courage, resilience, and the guidance of professionals versed in the intricacies of narcissistic abuse recovery.

UNDERSTANDING COMPLEX PTSD AND TRAUMA BONDING

Narcissistic abuse is a form of relational trauma, a prolonged and repetitive assault on the survivor's sense of self, autonomy, and emotional well-being. The psychological aftermath of this abuse often manifests as Complex Post-Traumatic Stress Disorder (C-PTSD), a condition characterized by a constellation of symptoms that extend far beyond the traditional conceptualization of PTSD.

While PTSD is commonly associated with a single, acute traumatic event, C-PTSD arises from chronic, sustained trauma, often inflicted by a trusted partner, parent, or caregiver. This betrayal of core relationships and the erosion of safety and security create a deep, pervasive sense of fear, mistrust, and emotional dysregulation that permeates every aspect of the survivor's life.

Symptoms of C-PTSD can include intrusive thoughts, flashbacks, dissociation, emotional numbing, and a persistent state of hypervigilance – all consequences of the survivor's nervous system being stuck in a perpetual state of fight-or-flight. Additionally, C-PTSD can manifest as negative self-perception, difficulty with interpersonal relationships, and a profound sense of detachment or emotional constriction.

Compounding the psychological impacts of C-PTSD is the insidious phenomenon of trauma bonding – a powerful emotional attachment that develops between the survivor and their abuser. This bond is forged through the cyclical nature of narcissistic abuse, where periods of idealization and love-bombing are punctuated by devaluation, cruelty, and intermittent reinforcement.

The survivor's brain, hardwired to seek patterns and form attachments, becomes conditioned to associate the narcissist's occasional kindness with relief from the abuse, creating a potent neurochemical reward system. This trauma bond can make it extraordinarily difficult for survivors to extricate themselves from the abusive dynamic, as their emotional and physiological responses become entangled with the perpetrator of their trauma.

Understanding the complexities of C-PTSD and trauma bonding is crucial for survivors as they navigate the healing process. By recognizing the root causes of their psychological and emotional turmoil, they can begin to dismantle the cognitive distortions and physiological dysregulation that have taken hold, paving the way for true recovery and self-reclamation.

STRATEGIES FOR MANAGING TRIGGERS AND FLASHBACKS

One of the most overwhelming aspects of C-PTSD is the persistent presence of triggers – external stimuli or internal experiences that can precipitate intrusive thoughts, emotional dysregulation, or full-blown flashbacks. These triggers can be seemingly innocuous – a particular scent, a familiar phrase, or even a specific time of day – but they have the power to transport the survivor back to the depths of their trauma, eroding their sense of safety and grounding in the present moment.

Managing these triggers and flashbacks is a critical component of the healing process, as they can perpetuate the cycle of hypervigilance, avoidance behaviors, and emotional distress that characterize C-PTSD. Fortunately, there are several evidence-based strategies that survivors can employ to mitigate the impact of these intrusive experiences.

Grounding Techniques

Grounding techniques are designed to anchor the survivor in the present moment, counteracting the dissociative state that often accompanies flashbacks and intrusive thoughts. These techniques can involve engaging the five senses – sight, sound, smell, taste, and touch – to redirect the mind's focus and create a sense of embodied awareness.

Examples of grounding exercises include:

- Descriptive breathing: Inhaling slowly while noticing the sensation of air entering the lungs, and exhaling while describing the experience aloud or mentally.

- Physical anchors: Gripping a textured object, digging one's feet into the ground, or splashing cold water on the face to reconnect with tangible sensations.

- Mindful observation: Visually taking in the surroundings, naming objects and colors, or focusing on intricate details in the environment.

These techniques, when practiced regularly, can help survivors cultivate a sense of safety and control, providing a foundation for managing the overwhelming emotions that often accompany trauma triggers.

Trauma-Informed Mindfulness

Mindfulness practices, when adapted to account for the unique needs of trauma survivors, can be powerful tools for regulating the physiological and emotional responses that underlie C-PTSD. By cultivating present-moment awareness and non-judgmental acceptance, mindfulness can help survivors disengage from the cyclical thought patterns and emotional reactivity that often exacerbate trauma symptoms.

Trauma-informed mindfulness incorporates principles of safety, choice, and empowerment, recognizing that traditional mindfulness practices may inadvertently trigger or overwhelm survivors in certain circumstances. Modifications may include:

- Providing options for open or closed-eye practices

- Emphasizing body awareness without explicitly focusing on sensations that could be triggering

- Offering alternative anchors (visual, auditory) for those who find breath awareness too overwhelming

- Encouraging self-compassion and acceptance of emotional experiences without judgment

When integrated into a comprehensive treatment plan, trauma-informed mindfulness can help survivors develop greater emotional regulation, reduce avoidance behaviors, and foster a sense of agency and self-acceptance in the face of their traumatic experiences.

EMDR and Somatic Therapies

Eye Movement Desensitization and Reprocessing (EMDR) and somatic therapies are specialized approaches that directly target the physiological and neurological impacts of trauma. EMDR, in particular, has been widely researched and recognized as an effective treatment for PTSD and C-PTSD, utilizing bilateral stimulation (eye movements, taps, or tones) to facilitate the reprocessing of traumatic memories and reduce their emotional intensity.

Somatic therapies, on the other hand, focus on the mind-body connection, recognizing that trauma is often encoded in the physical form through muscular tension, postural patterns, and dysregulated autonomic functions. Techniques such as somatic experiencing, sensorimotor psychotherapy, and trauma-sensitive yoga can help survivors reconnect with their bodies, release stored trauma energy, and regain a sense of embodied safety and self-regulation.

While these modalities often require the guidance of trained professionals, they offer powerful avenues for addressing the deeply ingrained physiological and neurological impacts of narcissistic abuse, complementing more traditional talk therapies and cognitive-behavioral interventions.

THE ROLE OF PROFESSIONAL SUPPORT

While the strategies outlined above can be invaluable tools in the survivor's healing journey, the complexities of C-PTSD and the profound psychological impacts of narcissistic abuse often necessitate the involvement of professional support systems. Therapists, counselors, and specialized support groups can provide the expertise, guidance, and validation that are essential for navigating the treacherous terrain of trauma recovery.

Trauma-Informed Psychotherapy

Working with a therapist who is well-versed in the dynamics of narcissistic abuse and the intricacies of C-PTSD can be a game-changer for survivors. These professionals possess a deep understanding of the manipulation tactics employed by narcissists, the cognitive distortions that often accompany trauma bonding, and the multifaceted psychological and emotional impacts on the survivor.

Trauma-informed psychotherapy approaches, such as cognitive processing therapy (CPT), prolonged exposure therapy (PE), and dialectical behavior therapy (DBT), can help survivors process their traumatic experiences, challenge distorted beliefs, and develop coping strategies for managing triggers, intrusive thoughts, and emotional dysregulation.

Additionally, therapists can provide a safe, non-judgmental space for survivors to explore their experiences, validate their emotions, and work through the complex grief and loss that often accompanies the dissolution of an abusive relationship – even when that relationship was profoundly toxic.

Specialized Support Groups

While individual therapy can be invaluable, the power of shared experience and validation within a support group setting cannot be overstated. Narcissistic abuse survivors often grapple with profound feelings of isolation, self-doubt, and the belief that their experiences are unique or unrelatable. Support groups can shatter this illusion, fostering a sense of community and connection with others who have walked a similar path.

In these groups, facilitated by trained professionals or seasoned survivors, participants can share their stories, process their emotions, and receive feedback and guidance from those who truly understand the complexities of narcissistic abuse. The normalization of experiences and the recognition that one is not alone in their struggles can be profoundly healing, counteracting the gaslighting and invalidation that were so prevalent during the abusive relationship.

Furthermore, support groups can provide a safe space for practicing new coping strategies, role-playing healthy boundary-setting, and

celebrating milestones in the recovery journey – all within a supportive
and empathetic environment.

Online Communities and Resources

For those who may face geographic or logistical barriers to accessing
in-person support, the digital realm offers a wealth of resources and
online communities dedicated to narcissistic abuse recovery. Social
media groups, forums, and specialized websites can provide a virtual
haven for survivors, offering a constant source of information, support,
and connection.

While online resources should never be a complete substitute for
professional support, they can complement traditional therapeutic
interventions by providing a sense of validation, community, and
access to a wealth of educational materials and personal accounts from
fellow survivors.

Additionally, many reputable organizations and therapists now offer virtual counseling services, allowing survivors to access trauma-informed care from the comfort and safety of their own homes.

The journey of unpacking the trauma inflicted by narcissistic abuse is a challenging and multifaceted endeavor, but one that can ultimately lead to profound healing, growth, and self-reclamation. By understanding the complexities of C-PTSD and trauma bonding, employing evidence-based strategies for managing triggers and flashbacks, and embracing the guidance and support of professionals and fellow survivors, those who have endured this insidious form of abuse can reclaim their sense of agency, autonomy, and worthiness.

It is a path that demands courage, resilience, and an unwavering commitment to self-compassion, but the rewards of this transformative journey are immeasurable – a newfound sense of freedom, authenticity, and the ability to author a narrative of empowerment and personal growth from the ashes of trauma.

CHAPTER 5

REBUILDING SELF-WORTH

At the core of narcissistic abuse lies a systematic erosion of the survivor's sense of self-worth. Through a relentless barrage of criticism, gaslighting, and emotional manipulation, the narcissist plants insidious seeds of doubt, shame, and self-loathing that take root deep within the psyche of their victim. The very essence of who the survivor is – their values, talents, and intrinsic worth – becomes distorted and suppressed beneath the weight of the abuser's dehumanizing narratives.

The process of reclaiming one's self-worth after enduring such profound psychological and emotional trauma is akin to excavating buried treasure – a painstaking, layer-by-layer unearthing of the authentic self that has been obscured by the rubble of abuse. It is a journey that demands unwavering self-compassion, a willingness to confront and challenge deeply ingrained negative beliefs, and a steadfast commitment to rediscovering the unique tapestry of strengths, passions, and aspirations that make each survivor whole.

CHALLENGING INTERNALIZED CRITICISM AND NEGATIVE BELIEFS

One of the most insidious legacies of narcissistic abuse is the internalization of the abuser's criticisms and negative narratives. These internalized beliefs become like a cruel inner voice, echoing the devaluing and demeaning messages that the survivor endured for so long. "You're not good enough," "You'll never amount to anything," "You're lucky anyone puts up with you" – these toxic mantras can play on a perpetual loop, sabotaging self-confidence, undermining personal growth, and perpetuating a cycle of self-doubt and self-loathing.

To rebuild self-worth, survivors must first identify and challenge these internalized beliefs, shining a light on their distorted origins and countering them with evidence-based affirmations of their inherent worth.

Cognitive Restructuring

Cognitive restructuring is a therapeutic technique that involves identifying and examining irrational, negative thought patterns and replacing them with more balanced, rational perspectives. For survivors of narcissistic abuse, this process often begins by recognizing the abuser's fingerprints on their self-critical inner dialogue.

Through journaling, counseling, or guided exercises, survivors can learn to separate the abuser's voice from their own authentic thoughts and feelings. Each negative belief or criticism can be dissected, its validity questioned, and its roots traced back to the manipulation tactics employed by the narcissist.

Once these distorted beliefs are exposed for what they are - remnants of psychological abuse rather than objective truths - survivors can begin the process of reframing their self-perceptions. This may involve compiling evidence that contradicts the negative beliefs, seeking input and validation from trusted loved ones, or simply practicing self-affirmations that counter the internalized criticisms.

Thought-Stopping and Redirection

Thought-stopping and redirection are complementary techniques that can be employed to disrupt the cyclical patterns of negative self-talk and internalized criticism. When a survivor recognizes that they are engaging in self-critical or self-deprecating thought patterns, they can actively interrupt these thoughts by issuing a mental "stop" command or visualizing a physical barrier.

Once the negative thought cycle is disrupted, the survivor can then consciously redirect their focus to more positive, affirming self-statements or engage in grounding exercises that anchor them in the present moment. This practice not only challenges the validity of the internalized criticisms but also reinforces the survivor's ability to exercise control over their thought patterns and self-perceptions.

AFFIRMATIONS AND SELF-COMPASSION EXERCISES

Rebuilding self-worth is not merely an intellectual exercise; it requires a deep emotional and spiritual reintegration of self-love, self-acceptance, and self-compassion. Affirmations and self-compassion exercises can serve as powerful tools in this transformative process, helping survivors to cultivate a profound sense of worthiness and unconditional positive regard for themselves.

Positive Affirmations

Affirmations are simple, present-tense statements that reinforce desired beliefs, attitudes, or behaviors. For survivors of narcissistic abuse, positive affirmations can act as a counterweight to the negative self-talk and internalized criticisms that have become deeply ingrained.

Examples of affirmations for rebuilding self-worth may include:

- "I am worthy of love, respect, and happiness."

- "I have innate value that no one can diminish or take away."

- "I am resilient, strong, and capable of overcoming challenges."

- "My worth is not defined by the opinions or actions of others."

- "I am on a journey of self-discovery and growth, and I embrace the process."

Affirmations can be spoken aloud, written in a journal, or incorporated into daily routines through the use of sticky notes, screensavers, or voice memos. The act of repeatedly affirming these positive statements can help to rewire neural pathways and reinforce a more compassionate, self-accepting inner dialogue.

Self-Compassion Meditations and Exercises

Self-compassion is a critical component of rebuilding self-worth, as it involves treating oneself with the same kindness, understanding, and support that one would extend to a beloved friend. For survivors of narcissistic abuse, who have endured relentless criticism and emotional invalidation, cultivating self-compassion can be a radical act of self-love and healing.

Self-compassion meditations and exercises can take many forms, but they typically involve practices that foster mindfulness, self-kindness, and a recognition of our shared human experience. Examples may include:

- Loving-kindness meditations: Silently repeating phrases of compassion and well-wishes toward oneself and others.

- Self-compassion break: Pausing in moments of self-criticism or struggle to acknowledge one's pain, offer words of kindness and understanding, and recognize that imperfection is part of the human experience.

- Writing a letter to oneself: Crafting a compassionate, supportive letter from the perspective of an unconditionally loving friend or family member.

- Self-compassion journaling: Reflecting on challenges, setbacks, or personal struggles with a lens of self-kindness and non-judgment.

As survivors practice self-compassion, they begin to internalize a sense of worthiness that extends beyond external validation or achievement. They learn to embrace their imperfections, honor their emotional experiences, and offer themselves the same empathy and care that they so freely give to others.

REDISCOVERING YOUR IDENTITY BEYOND THE ABUSE

For many survivors of narcissistic abuse, their sense of identity became inextricably intertwined with the abusive relationship and the narratives imposed upon them by the narcissist. Their values, aspirations, and even hobbies or interests may have been suppressed or eroded as the abuser exerted control and dominance over their lives.

Rediscovering one's identity beyond the confines of the abuse is a critical aspect of rebuilding self-worth. It involves a profound process of self-exploration, reconnecting with the authentic aspects of oneself that existed before the trauma, and cultivating new dimensions of identity that align with one's values, strengths, and innate passions.

Reconnecting with Past Passions and Interests

For many survivors, the road to rediscovering their identity begins with revisiting the hobbies, creative pursuits, or interests that once brought them joy and fulfillment before the abusive relationship took hold. Whether it was painting, writing, playing a musical instrument, or engaging in a particular sport or activity, reconnecting with these long-dormant passions can reignite a sense of purpose, self-expression, and intrinsic motivation.

Engaging in these pursuits not only provides a healthy outlet for processing emotions and exploring one's creativity but also serves as a powerful reminder of the authentic aspects of oneself that existed before the trauma of abuse. It is a reclamation of identity, a defiant act of self-nurturance that reinforces the survivor's worth and autonomy.

Exploring New Avenues of Growth and Self-Discovery

While reconnecting with past passions can be a powerful starting point, rebuilding self-worth often involves venturing into new realms of self-discovery and personal growth. This may involve exploring new hobbies, learning new skills, or immersing oneself in educational or cultural experiences that challenge limiting beliefs and expand one's horizons.

For some survivors, this exploration may take the form of pursuing long-held dreams or goals that were suppressed during the abusive relationship. Enrolling in a course of study, starting a business, or traveling to a place they've always longed to visit can reignite a sense of agency, ambition, and self-determination that was once stifled by the narcissist's control.

Others may find solace and self-discovery in practices like journaling, meditation, or engaging with spiritual or philosophical traditions that resonate with their values and provide a deeper sense of meaning and purpose.

Ultimately, the process of rediscovering one's identity is a highly personal journey, one that involves shedding the limiting narratives imposed by the abuser and embracing the multifaceted, ever-evolving tapestry of one's authentic self.

Embracing Imperfection and Redefining Strength

Throughout the journey of rebuilding self-worth, survivors must confront and redefine their understanding of what it means to be "strong" or "perfect." The narcissist's distorted narratives often propagate unrealistic and damaging expectations of infallibility, perpetuating the belief that any flaw, mistake, or vulnerability is a sign of weakness or inadequacy.

In reality, true strength lies in the ability to embrace one's imperfections, to accept that growth and self-discovery are ongoing processes rife with stumbles and setbacks. It involves cultivating self-compassion, resilience, and the courage to be authentically oneself – flaws, quirks, and all.

Redefining strength also means rejecting the narcissist's narrow and toxic conceptualizations of power and dominance. True strength is not found in the subjugation or devaluation of others; it is embodied in the ability to lift others up, to lead with empathy and kindness, and to create spaces where everyone's worth is honored and celebrated.

As survivors shed the narcissist's distorted narratives and embrace their authentic selves, they come to realize that their worth is not contingent upon perfection or the validation of others. It is an intrinsic, unassailable quality that radiates from within, a beacon of self-love and self-acceptance that cannot be diminished by the cruelty or manipulation of others.

The journey of rebuilding self-worth after narcissistic abuse is a transformative odyssey, one that demands immense courage, self-compassion, and a steadfast commitment to personal growth and self-discovery. It is a process of excavating the authentic self that has been buried beneath the rubble of emotional trauma, of challenging the internalized criticisms and distorted narratives that have taken root, and of cultivating a profound sense of worthiness that transcends external validation or achievement.

Through this journey, survivors not only reclaim their sense of identity and self-love but also emerge as beacons of resilience and strength – living embodiments of the indomitable human spirit's capacity to rise from the ashes of even the most insidious forms of abuse.

And as they embrace their worth, their passions, and their authentic selves, survivors pave the way for a life of profound fulfillment, purpose, and unapologetic self-expression – a life where their voices are no longer silenced, their dreams are no longer deferred, and their inherent value shines brighter than ever before.

PART 3

THRIVING AFTER ABUSE

CHAPTER 6

HEALTHY BOUNDARIES AND RELATIONSHIPS

As survivors of narcissistic abuse embark on the journey of rebuilding their lives, the quest for healthy relationships and a strong support system becomes paramount. The manipulation tactics and emotional exploitation they endured have likely left deep scars, eroding their ability to establish and maintain boundaries, recognize toxic patterns, and discern genuine support from veiled forms of control.

Healing from the trauma of narcissistic abuse involves not only reclaiming one's sense of self-worth but also developing the skills and awareness necessary to cultivate nurturing connections, identify potential red flags, and build a network of individuals who honor and uplift their inherent value.

SETTING AND ENFORCING BOUNDARIES

Boundaries are the invisible lines that define our physical, emotional, and psychological limits – the demarcations that separate our authentic selves from the needs, demands, and intrusions of others. For survivors of narcissistic abuse, the concept of boundaries may feel foreign or even frightening, as the abuser's tactics often relied on the systematic erosion of these safeguards.

Reclaiming the ability to set and enforce healthy boundaries is a critical step in the healing process, as it empowers survivors to reclaim autonomy, self-respect, and a sense of agency over their lives.

Understanding Boundary Types

Boundaries can take many forms, encompassing various aspects of our lives and relationships. Some common types of boundaries include:

Physical Boundaries: Defining personal space, privacy, and physical touch preferences.

Emotional Boundaries: Protecting oneself from emotional manipulation, toxic behaviors, and invasive emotional demands.

Time and Energy Boundaries: Setting limits on how much time and energy is devoted to others, while reserving adequate resources for self-care and personal pursuits.

Material Boundaries: Establishing boundaries around personal possessions, finances, and shared resources.

Intellectual Boundaries: Respecting differing beliefs, values, and opinions without compromising one's own convictions.

Identifying Personal Boundaries

Before boundaries can be effectively communicated and enforced, survivors must first engage in a process of self-reflection to identify their personal limits and needs. This may involve journaling, seeking guidance from a therapist or counselor, or simply tuning into one's intuition and emotional responses to various situations.

- What behaviors or actions from others make me feel uncomfortable, drained, or disrespected?

- What aspects of my life or personal space do I need to protect or limit access to?

- What beliefs, values, or identities are non-negotiable for me, and how can I uphold them in my relationships?

- How much time and energy can I realistically devote to others without compromising my well-being?

By gaining clarity on their boundaries, survivors can begin to articulate them in a clear, assertive manner, paving the way for healthier interactions and relationships.

Communicating and Enforcing Boundaries

Once personal boundaries have been identified, the next step is to communicate them effectively to others. This may involve having direct conversations with loved ones, setting ground rules in professional or social settings, or simply asserting limits in the moment when boundaries are crossed.

Effective boundary communication often involves:

- Using "I" statements to convey personal needs and limits without blaming or accusing others.

- Being specific and direct about the behaviors or situations that are unacceptable.

- Explaining the reasons behind the boundary, if appropriate, to foster understanding and cooperation.

- Remaining calm and respectful, even in the face of push-back or resistance.

Enforcing boundaries is equally crucial, as boundaries without consequences or follow-through lose their potency. Survivors may need to implement measures such as removing themselves from situations where boundaries are violated, establishing consequences for repeated infractions, or, in extreme cases, limiting or severing contact with individuals who consistently disrespect their limits.

Building the Muscle Memory of Boundary-Setting

Like any new skill, boundary-setting requires practice and repetition to become second nature. Survivors may encounter challenges such as guilt, fear of conflict, or doubts about their right to assert boundaries. It is essential to approach this process with self-compassion, recognizing that it is a journey of personal growth and empowerment.

Engaging in role-playing exercises, seeking support from a therapist or support group, and celebrating small victories along the way can reinforce the "muscle memory" of boundary-setting and foster a sense of confidence in asserting one's needs.

Over time, the act of upholding boundaries becomes a powerful affirmation of self-worth and autonomy, a tangible manifestation of the survivor's commitment to creating a life defined by respect, integrity, and self-preservation.

RED FLAGS IN NEW RELATIONSHIPS

As survivors begin to navigate the world of new relationships, whether romantic, professional, or social, it is crucial to remain vigilant for potential red flags that may signal the presence of toxic or narcissistic patterns. The trauma of past abuse can create blind spots or a tendency to overlook or rationalize concerning behaviors, making it imperative to cultivate a heightened awareness and trust in one's instincts.

While every situation is unique, there are certain universal red flags that survivors should be attuned to, as they may indicate the potential for future manipulation, control, or emotional exploitation.

Love-Bombing and Idealization

The narcissist's playbook often begins with a tactic known as love-bombing – an overwhelming deluge of affection, attention, and idealization designed to sweep the target off their feet and create a powerful emotional bond. While this intense courtship can be intoxicating, it is essential to recognize it as a potential red flag, as it may foreshadow a cycle of devaluation and abuse.

Survivors should be wary of relationships that move at an alarmingly rapid pace, with declarations of deep connection or commitment before genuine trust and intimacy have been established. Healthy relationships unfold gradually, with a natural ebb and flow that allows for genuine familiarity and mutual understanding to develop.

Boundary Violations and Disrespect

A fundamental aspect of healthy relationships is the mutual respect for personal boundaries and limits. Any individual who consistently disregards or violates stated boundaries, whether physical, emotional, or otherwise, should be viewed as a potential red flag.

This may manifest as persistent boundary-pushing, manipulation tactics to erode boundaries, or outright disregard for the survivor's expressed needs or comfort levels. Such behaviors often signal a lack of respect for the survivor's autonomy and a potential precursor to more severe forms of control or emotional abuse.

Gaslighting and Reality Distortion

Gaslighting, the insidious tactic of undermining another person's perception of reality, is a hallmark of narcissistic abuse. Survivors should be attuned to any behaviors or statements that call into question their memories, experiences, or intuition, as these may be early indicators of gaslighting tendencies.

Reality distortion can also manifest as blatant lying, inconsistent narratives, or attempts to rewrite history – all designed to sow seeds of confusion and self-doubt within the survivor. Recognizing these patterns early on can prevent further entanglement with individuals who may ultimately seek to erode the survivor's sense of reality and self-trust.

Lack of Accountability and Blame-Shifting

Healthy relationships involve a willingness to take accountability for one's actions, acknowledge mistakes, and engage in constructive conflict resolution. Individuals who consistently deflect responsibility, shift blame onto others, or refuse to acknowledge their role in conflicts or misunderstandings may be exhibiting narcissistic tendencies.

This lack of accountability often goes hand-in-hand with a sense of entitlement or a belief that the individual is above reproach or criticism. Survivors should be wary of anyone who consistently portrays themselves as the perpetual victim or who refuses to engage in self-reflection or personal growth.

Isolation Tactics and Control

One of the most insidious tactics employed by narcissists is the systematic isolation of their victims from support systems and external sources of validation or alternative perspectives. Survivors should be alert to any attempts to separate them from loved ones, discredit trusted confidants, or limit their access to resources or social connections.

Additionally, any behaviors or demands that seek to exert excessive control over the survivor's time, activities, or personal choices should be viewed as a significant red flag, as they may be indicative of a desire for dominance and subjugation.

BUILDING A SUPPORTIVE NETWORK

While recognizing and avoiding toxic patterns is crucial, an equally important aspect of fostering healthy relationships is intentionally cultivating a network of supportive, nurturing connections. This support system serves as a bulwark against future manipulation, a source of validation and affirmation, and a safe haven for the survivor to continue their journey of healing and personal growth.

Identifying Healthy Support Sources

A robust support network often comprises a diverse array of individuals, each serving unique roles and providing different forms of nurturing. Some potential sources of healthy support include:

Trusted Friends and Family: Those who have demonstrated unwavering compassion, respect for boundaries, and a willingness to listen without judgment or manipulation.

Support Groups: Peer-led or professionally facilitated groups that foster connection, validation, and shared experiences among survivors of narcissistic abuse or other forms of trauma.

Mentors or Role Models: Individuals who embody the qualities of resilience, self-worth, and healthy relationships, serving as inspiring examples for the survivor's growth.

Therapists or Counselors: Trained professionals who can provide guidance, objective perspectives, and evidence-based strategies for healing and personal development.

Online Communities: Virtual spaces where survivors can connect, share resources, and find solace in the shared experiences of others on similar journeys.

Cultivating Reciprocal, Nurturing Bonds

As survivors begin to forge new connections, it is essential to prioritize relationships built on mutual respect, reciprocity, and a shared commitment to personal growth and emotional well-being. These nurturing bonds should foster a sense of safety, acceptance, and empowerment, allowing the survivor to engage authentically without fear of judgment, invalidation, or exploitation.

Reciprocity is a key aspect of healthy relationships, where both parties actively contribute to the emotional bank account of the connection through acts of kindness, attentive listening, and a genuine interest in each other's lives and experiences.

Building Trust and Setting Realistic Expectations

After enduring the betrayal and emotional manipulation of narcissistic abuse, survivors may understandably struggle with trust issues or harbor unrealistic expectations of perfection in their newfound connections. It is essential to approach the process of building trust with patience and realistic expectations, recognizing that healthy relationships involve a gradual unfolding of vulnerability and mutual understanding.

Setting boundaries around personal limits, communicating needs and expectations openly, and allowing trust to develop organically can help foster a sense of emotional safety and mitigate the risk of repeating

past patterns of idealization or codependency.

Role of Support Networks in Ongoing Healing

A robust support network extends far beyond the initial stages of

healing from narcissistic abuse. As survivors continue on their journey

of personal growth and self-discovery, their nurturing connections can

serve as a source of ongoing encouragement, accountability, and

celebration of milestones.

Support networks can provide a safe space for survivors to process

setbacks or challenges, seek guidance during times of uncertainty, and

share in the joys and triumphs of their evolving journeys. They can also

serve as a powerful reminder of the survivor's inherent worth and

resilience, counteracting any residual self-doubt or internalized

narratives from the abusive past.

By intentionally cultivating a network of healthy, reciprocal

relationships, survivors not only safeguard themselves against future exploitation but also create a tapestry of connections that nourish their spirits, reinforce their boundaries, and empower them to thrive in authenticity and self-acceptance.

The journey towards healthy boundaries and nurturing relationships is a transformative one, demanding vigilance, self-awareness, and a willingness to embrace personal growth. As survivors navigate this terrain, they not only reclaim their autonomy and self-worth but also lay the foundations for a life rich in meaningful connections, emotional intimacy, and a profound sense of belonging.

It is a path that requires courage, resilience, and a steadfast commitment to honoring oneself and the inherent value of authentic human bonds. Yet, with each step taken, survivors emerge as beacons of empowerment, their boundaries fortified, their discernment sharpened, and their capacity for genuine connection amplified.

For it is within the embrace of a thriving support network and the sanctuary of healthy relationships that the true essence of healing unfolds - a reclamation of trust, a celebration of vulnerability, and a

defiant affirmation that one's worth is not defined by the cruelty of the

past but by the richness of connections yet to be forged.

CHAPTER 7

PERSONAL GROWTH AND

EMPOWERMENT

The path to healing from narcissistic abuse is not merely a journey of recovery; it is a transformative odyssey of personal growth and empowerment. As survivors shed the shackles of emotional manipulation and reclaim their sense of self-worth, they are presented with a profound opportunity – the chance to author a new narrative, one defined not by the trauma they have endured but by the resilience, wisdom, and authentic self-expression they have cultivated in its wake.

This chapter serves as a roadmap for that odyssey, illuminating the path towards pursuing one's passions, nurturing emotional intelligence, and embracing the transformative power of forgiveness and release. It is a call to embrace the profound growth that can emerge from adversity, to harness the lessons gleaned from pain, and to chart a course towards a life imbued with purpose, meaning, and an unshakable sense of personal empowerment.

Pursuing Passions, Goals, and Meaning

For many survivors of narcissistic abuse, the relentless emotional manipulation and control they endured left them disconnected from their deepest passions, aspirations, and sense of purpose. The narcissist's tactics often involved the systematic suppression of their victim's autonomy, ambitions, and independent pursuits, reducing them to mere extensions of the abuser's desires and narratives.

As survivors embark on their journey of reclamation, rediscovering and nurturing their inherent passions becomes a powerful act of self-affirmation and personal growth. It is a defiant declaration that their worth and fulfillment are no longer tethered to the validation or approval of their abuser but are instead anchored within the authentic expression of their unique gifts, talents, and callings.

Reigniting Dormant Passions

For some survivors, the path to rediscovering their passions may involve revisiting long-dormant interests, creative pursuits, or hobbies that once brought them joy and a sense of purpose. Whether it is painting, writing, gardening, or engaging in a particular sport or artistic endeavor, reigniting these passions can serve as a potent catalyst for personal growth and self-exploration.

Not only do these pursuits provide a healthy outlet for processing emotions and channeling creative energy, but they also offer a tangible reminder of the inherent strengths and talents that existed within the survivor long before the trauma of abuse took hold. Reclaiming these passions is an act of reclamation, a symbolic shedding of the limiting narratives imposed by the narcissist and an affirmation of the survivor's multifaceted identity.

Pursuing New Dreams and Aspirations

For others, the journey may involve embarking on entirely new paths, exploring uncharted territories of personal growth and self-discovery.

This could manifest as pursuing long-held dreams or ambitions that were suppressed or dismissed during the abusive relationship, such as returning to education, starting a business, or embarking on a transformative travel experience.

Embracing these new aspirations is not merely a matter of checking boxes or achieving external milestones; it is a profound act of self-actualization, a declaration that the survivor's worth and potential are not confined to the limiting narratives of the past but are instead boundless, ever-evolving expressions of their authentic selves.

Cultivating a Sense of Purpose and Meaning

Inherent in the pursuit of passions and aspirations is the cultivation of a deeper sense of purpose and meaning – an anchor that grounds the survivor's journey and imbues their efforts with profound significance. This sense of purpose can emerge from a variety of sources, such as engaging in work or causes that align with one's values, exploring spirituality or philosophical traditions, or simply committing to a path of continuous growth and self-discovery.

As survivors connect with this sense of purpose, they begin to transcend the emotional turmoil of the past and embrace a more expansive perspective on their lives and experiences. The trauma they endured is no longer the defining narrative but rather a crucible from which they have forged a deeper understanding of their resilience, their innate worth, and their capacity to create meaning and fulfillment on their own terms.

DEVELOPING RESILIENCE AND EMOTIONAL INTELLIGENCE

Narcissistic abuse is a form of relational trauma that can leave deep scars on the emotional and psychological landscape of its survivors. To truly thrive in the aftermath of this experience, cultivating resilience and emotional intelligence becomes not merely a luxury but a necessity – a suite of skills and capacities that equip survivors to navigate life's challenges with grace, self-awareness, and an unwavering commitment to personal growth.

Building Emotional Agility

Emotional agility refers to the ability to navigate one's inner emotional world with flexibility, self-awareness, and a willingness to experience and process a full range of feelings without becoming overwhelmed or reactive. For survivors of narcissistic abuse, who have often been conditioned to suppress or invalidate their emotional experiences, developing this agility can be a transformative process.

Practices such as mindfulness meditation, journaling, and therapeutic interventions like dialectical behavior therapy (DBT) can help survivors learn to observe their emotions with curiosity and non-judgment, recognizing that all feelings are transient and that their inherent worth is not contingent upon any particular emotional state.

As survivors cultivate emotional agility, they become less entrapped by the cyclical patterns of self-criticism, shame, or reactivity that once defined their inner landscapes. Instead, they develop the capacity to respond to life's challenges with presence, self-compassion, and a deeper understanding of their own emotional needs and boundaries.

Fostering Resilience through Growth Mindset

Resilience is not merely a trait but a cultivated capacity – a muscle that is strengthened through embracing a growth mindset and a commitment to continuous learning and adaptation. For survivors of narcissistic abuse, who have endured profound adversity and likely internalized narratives of inadequacy or helplessness, fostering resilience becomes a powerful act of personal empowerment.

A growth mindset involves recognizing that challenges and setbacks are not permanent states but opportunities for growth, learning, and the development of new skills and perspectives. It involves reframing failure not as a reflection of inherent worth but as a natural part of the journey towards mastery and self-discovery.

As survivors embrace this growth mindset, they begin to view their experiences through a lens of post-traumatic growth, recognizing that the very adversity they have faced has equipped them with a depth of resilience, wisdom, and self-awareness that can serve as a wellspring of strength in navigating future obstacles.

Developing Empathy and Emotional Intelligence

Emotional intelligence encompasses not only the ability to navigate one's inner emotional landscape but also the capacity to attune to and resonate with the experiences of others. For survivors of narcissistic abuse, who have often been conditioned to prioritize the emotional needs and narratives of their abuser over their own, reclaiming empathy and emotional intelligence can be a profound act of self-reclamation.

Through practices such as active listening, perspective-taking, and cultivating compassion for the shared human experience, survivors can begin to rebuild their capacity for healthy emotional attunement and connection. They can learn to honor their own emotional boundaries while simultaneously developing a deeper appreciation for the richness and complexity of the emotional worlds of those around them.

This emotional intelligence not only fosters more fulfilling and authentic relationships but also serves as a wellspring of self-awareness and personal growth. As survivors deepen their attunement to the emotional experiences of others, they gain greater insight into their own emotional landscapes, cultivating a more nuanced understanding of their needs, triggers, and paths towards self-regulation and healing.

FORGIVENESS AND LETTING GO

For many survivors of narcissistic abuse, the concept of forgiveness can be a complex and emotionally charged terrain. The depth of the trauma they have endured, the betrayal of trust, and the lasting scars of manipulation can make the idea of forgiveness feel like a monumental, seemingly insurmountable challenge.

Yet, as survivors progress on their journey of personal growth and empowerment, they may come to recognize that forgiveness is not merely a gift bestowed upon their abusers but a profound act of self-love and release - a conscious decision to shed the emotional burdens that have weighed upon them and to reclaim their innate capacity for joy, peace, and authentic connection.

Understanding the Dimensions of Forgiveness

Forgiveness is a multifaceted concept that encompasses various dimensions, each with its own nuances and implications for the healing process. These dimensions may include:

Self-Forgiveness: Releasing the shame, guilt, and self-criticism that often accompany the experience of being a victim of abuse. This involves cultivating self-compassion and recognizing that one's worth is not diminished by the actions of others.

Forgiveness of the Abuser: This does not necessarily imply condoning the abusive behavior or maintaining contact with the narcissist but rather a conscious decision to release the emotional weight of resentment, anger, and a desire for vengeance or retribution.

Forgiveness of Others: In many cases, narcissistic abuse can involve the complicity or enabling behaviors of others, whether intentional or not. Forgiveness in this context involves releasing the judgments and grievances towards those who may have played a role, however peripheral, in the survivor's trauma.

Forgiveness as a Process, Not an Event

It is essential to recognize that forgiveness is not a singular event but rather an ongoing process - a journey of self-reflection, emotional release, and a conscious choice to shed the burdens that no longer serve one's growth and well-being. This process may involve a range of emotions, from anger and grief to compassion and acceptance, and it unfolds at its own unique pace for each individual.

For some survivors, forgiveness may manifest as a gradual easing of resentment or a newfound ability to view their abuser with a sense of detachment or even empathy for the psychological and emotional wounds that may have driven their behavior. For others, forgiveness may involve a more decisive act of release, a symbolic or ritual letting go of the pain and trauma that has been carried for so long.

Regardless of the form it takes, forgiveness is a journey, not a destination – a continuous process of self-discovery, emotional healing, and a commitment to living a life imbued with greater freedom, joy, and authenticity.

Forgiveness and Personal Empowerment

Ultimately, the act of forgiveness is not about absolving the abuser of responsibility or minimizing the harm they have inflicted. Rather, it is a profound act of personal empowerment – a reclamation of one's inherent worth and a refusal to allow the weight of past traumas to define or limit one's present reality.

As survivors embrace forgiveness, they begin to shed the emotional shackles that have bound them to their abusers, freeing themselves from the cyclical patterns of resentment, anger, and self-recrimination. In doing so, they create space for personal growth, emotional healing, and a deeper connection to their authentic selves – a self that is no longer tethered to the narratives of the past but is instead anchored in a present moment imbued with possibility, resilience, and an unwavering sense of self-worth.

The journey of personal growth and empowerment that unfolds in the wake of narcissistic abuse is a testament to the indomitable strength of the human spirit. It is a path that demands courage, self-compassion, and an unwavering commitment to embracing the lessons and wisdom that can emerge from even the darkest of adversities.

As survivors pursue their passions, cultivate emotional intelligence, and embrace the transformative power of forgiveness, they not only reclaim their sense of agency and self-determination but also become living embodiments of post-traumatic growth – beacons of resilience and inspiration for others who have endured similar trials.

It is a journey that challenges the limiting narratives imposed by the narcissist, defying the notion that one's worth is contingent upon external validation or achievement. Instead, it affirms that true empowerment emerges from within, a wellspring of authenticity, purpose, and an unshakable belief in one's inherent value as a human being.

And as survivors traverse this odyssey, they come to realize that the very trauma that once threatened to diminish them has, in fact, become the crucible from which they have forged a deeper sense of self-awareness, emotional mastery, and a profound appreciation for the richness and resilience of the human experience.

For in the end, personal growth and empowerment are not mere endpoints but a continuous spiral of evolution – a journey that transcends the confines of any single experience or circumstance and beckons us ever forward, toward a life imbued with meaning, connection, and a relentless pursuit of our truest, most authentic selves.

CHAPTER 8

MAINTAINING HEALING AND WISDOM

The journey to healing from narcissistic abuse is a profound and transformative process, but it is not a linear path. Like any recovery, there will be ups and downs, moments of triumph and moments of struggle. Maintaining the progress you've made and continuing to grow from the wisdom you've gained is crucial for long-term healing and thriving. This chapter will explore strategies for relapse prevention, ways to share your hard-earned lessons with others, and the profound role of post-traumatic growth in your life after abuse.

RELAPSE PREVENTION STRATEGIES

While the term "relapse" is often associated with addiction recovery, it can also apply to the healing process from emotional trauma. A relapse in this context refers to a temporary setback or regression in your healing journey, where old patterns of thinking, feeling, or behaving may resurface. It's important to understand that relapses are common and do not negate the progress you've made. However, being proactive and implementing effective relapse prevention strategies can help minimize their frequency and severity.

1.   Recognize Your Triggers and Warning Signs

One of the most powerful tools in relapse prevention is self-awareness. By becoming attuned to your personal triggers and warning signs, you can take preventative measures before a full-blown relapse occurs. Triggers can be external, such as encountering your abuser, hearing specific phrases they used, or being in environments that remind you of the abuse. Internal triggers can include negative thought patterns, emotional states like anger or depression, or physiological responses like anxiety or panic attacks.

Developing a comprehensive list of your triggers and associated warning signs can help you identify when you're at risk of a relapse.

This awareness allows you to implement coping strategies promptly, preventing a downward spiral.

2. Establish a Robust Support Network

A strong support network is invaluable in relapse prevention. Surround yourself with people who understand your healing journey, validate your experiences, and offer unconditional support. This network can include trusted friends, family members, therapists, support group members, or even online communities of fellow survivors.

When you feel yourself slipping or encountering triggers, reach out to your support system immediately. They can provide a listening ear, offer perspective, and remind you of the progress you've made. Having people who will hold you accountable and gently steer you back on track can make a significant difference in preventing or minimizing relapses.

3. Practice Self-Care and Stress Management

Stress and overwhelm can contribute significantly to the risk of relapse. When you're physically and emotionally drained, your resilience and coping mechanisms can become compromised, making you more vulnerable to negative thought patterns and emotional triggers.

Prioritizing self-care and implementing effective stress management techniques can help you maintain a sense of balance and equilibrium. This can include:

- Regular exercise and physical activity

- Mindfulness practices like meditation, deep breathing, or yoga

- Engaging in hobbies and activities that bring you joy

- Maintaining a nutritious diet and proper sleep hygiene

- Setting boundaries and learning to say "no" when necessary

- Seeking professional help when needed (therapy, coaching, etc.)

By taking care of your physical, emotional, and mental well-being, you build resilience and increase your capacity to navigate challenges without succumbing to a relapse.

4. Identify and Challenge Negative Self-Talk

Negative self-talk and limiting beliefs can be significant obstacles in maintaining your healing progress. These inner critics often echo the abusive messages you received during the narcissistic abuse, perpetuating feelings of inadequacy, shame, and self-doubt.

It's crucial to become aware of these negative thought patterns and actively challenge them. When you catch yourself engaging in self-criticism or catastrophizing, pause and evaluate the validity of those thoughts. Ask yourself:

- Is this thought based in reality, or is it a distortion?

- What evidence do I have to support or refute this belief?

- Would I say this to a loved one in a similar situation?

Replace negative self-talk with more balanced, compassionate, and realistic perspectives. Affirmations, journaling, and cognitive-behavioral techniques can help rewire these ingrained thought patterns and prevent relapses into self-doubt and self-sabotage.

5.   Embrace a Growth Mindset

A growth mindset is the belief that your abilities, skills, and personal qualities are not fixed but can be developed and improved through effort and perseverance. This mindset is particularly valuable in relapse prevention, as it allows you to view setbacks and challenges as opportunities for growth rather than failures.

When you encounter a relapse or struggle, approach it with curiosity and an open mind. Instead of berating yourself, ask:

- What can I learn from this experience?

- How can I approach this situation differently next time?

- What resources or support do I need to overcome this challenge?

Embracing a growth mindset fosters resilience, adaptability, and a willingness to continually learn and evolve. It transforms setbacks into stepping stones, propelling you forward on your healing journey.

PASSING ON LESSONS TO OTHERS

As you progress in your healing and gain invaluable wisdom from your experiences, a natural desire may arise to share your hard-earned lessons with others. Passing on your knowledge and insights can not only benefit fellow survivors but also contribute to societal awareness and understanding of narcissistic abuse.

1. Share Your Story

Your personal story of survival and recovery can be a powerful source of inspiration and hope for others navigating similar situations. Consider writing a memoir, starting a blog, or participating in speaking engagements or support groups to share your narrative.

When sharing your story, focus on the lessons learned, the strategies that helped you heal, and the personal growth you experienced. Remember that every survivor's journey is unique, so avoid comparing or minimizing others' experiences. Your story can serve as a beacon of hope, reminding others that healing is possible and that they are not alone.

2.   Become an Advocate

Narcissistic abuse and emotional manipulation often thrive in silence and societal misunderstanding. By becoming an advocate, you can raise awareness, challenge stigmas, and support systemic changes that protect and empower survivors.

Advocacy can take many forms, such as:

- Volunteering for or supporting organizations that provide resources for survivors

- Lobbying for policy changes or legislation that address narcissistic abuse

- Using social media platforms to educate and spread awareness

- Writing op-eds or articles for local or national publications

- Participating in community outreach programs or workshops

As an advocate, you can leverage your lived experience and knowledge to create positive change and ensure that others receive the support and resources they need.

3.   Mentor and Support Fellow Survivors

One of the most meaningful ways to pass on your lessons is by directly supporting and mentoring fellow survivors. Your empathy, understanding, and guidance can be invaluable for those navigating the early stages of their healing journey.

Consider volunteering as a peer mentor or facilitator in support groups, either in-person or online. Share your coping strategies, offer validation and encouragement, and serve as a living example of what is possible through perseverance and dedication to healing.

Remember, mentoring is a two-way street. As you support others, you may gain new insights and perspectives that deepen your own healing and wisdom.

THE ROLE OF POST-TRAUMATIC GROWTH

While the aftermath of narcissistic abuse can be devastating, many survivors report experiencing a profound sense of personal growth and transformation as they heal. This phenomenon, known as post-traumatic growth (PTG), refers to the positive psychological changes that can occur as a result of struggling with highly challenging life circumstances.

PTG is not about minimizing the trauma or suggesting that the abuse was somehow beneficial. Rather, it acknowledges the resilience and strength that can emerge from navigating and overcoming adversity.

Embracing the potential for post-traumatic growth can be a powerful source of motivation and meaning in your ongoing healing journey.

1.   Increased Self-Awareness and Resilience

Surviving narcissistic abuse often requires developing a deep well of inner strength, self-awareness, and resilience. Through the healing process, you may discover aspects of yourself that you never knew existed – an unwavering determination, a fierce independence, or a profound capacity for self-compassion.

This heightened self-awareness and resilience can translate into a greater sense of self-confidence and self-trust. You may find yourself better equipped to navigate future challenges, set healthy boundaries, and prioritize your well-being. The lessons learned from your trauma can become a potent source of strength and wisdom.

2.   Deeper Appreciation for Life and Relationships

The experience of narcissistic abuse can strip away the illusions and false narratives that once shaped your reality. As you heal, you may gain a renewed appreciation for the simple joys and meaningful connections in your life.

Relationships may take on a deeper significance, as you learn to cultivate authenticity, vulnerability, and mutual respect. You may find yourself gravitating towards people and experiences that align with your core values and bring genuine fulfillment.

This newfound appreciation can also extend to your relationship with yourself. You may develop a greater sense of self-love, self-acceptance, and gratitude for the journey that has shaped you into the person you are today.

3.   **Redefined Priorities and Purpose**

Trauma has a way of putting life into perspective and prompting a re-evaluation of priorities. As you emerge from the depths of narcissistic abuse, you may find that your values, goals, and sense of purpose have shifted.

Perhaps you've discovered a newfound passion for advocacy or helping others. Or maybe you've realized the importance of pursuing a career or lifestyle that aligns with your authentic self. Some survivors even report feeling a deeper sense of spirituality or connection to something larger than themselves.

This redefinition of priorities and purpose can imbue your life with renewed meaning and direction. You may feel more intentional about how you spend your time, energy, and resources, prioritizing what truly matters to you.

4.   Increased Empathy and Compassion

The pain and suffering endured during narcissistic abuse can cultivate a profound sense of empathy and compassion – not only for yourself but also for others who have experienced similar traumas.

As you heal, you may find yourself more attuned to the struggles and emotional experiences of those around you. This heightened empathy can foster deeper connections, stronger bonds, and a greater capacity for understanding and non-judgment.

Additionally, your journey may inspire a desire to extend compassion not only to others but also to yourself. Self-compassion can be a powerful antidote to the internalized criticism and shame often associated with abuse, allowing you to embrace your humanity and treat yourself with kindness and acceptance.

Embracing post-traumatic growth is not about minimizing the pain and suffering you've endured. Rather, it's about acknowledging the profound transformation that can occur when you navigate adversity with resilience, self-awareness, and a willingness to learn and grow. By embracing the potential for positive change, you can continue to deepen your healing, find meaning in your experiences, and pave the way for a life filled with purpose, fulfillment, and wisdom.

The journey of healing from narcissistic abuse is a lifelong process, one that requires vigilance, self-compassion, and a commitment to personal growth. By implementing effective relapse prevention strategies, sharing your hard-earned lessons with others, and embracing the role of post-traumatic growth, you can not only maintain your healing progress but also continue to thrive in ways you never thought possible.

Remember, healing is not a linear path, and setbacks are natural and expected. When you encounter obstacles or relapses, treat them as opportunities for learning and growth, rather than failures. Seek support from your network, practice self-care, and challenge negative self-talk with compassion and understanding.

As you continue on this journey, consider passing on your wisdom and insights to fellow survivors. Your story, advocacy efforts, and mentorship can provide hope, validation, and vital resources to those still navigating the early stages of healing.

Lastly, embrace the potential for post-traumatic growth. Your resilience, self-awareness, and renewed appreciation for life can serve as beacons of hope, reminding you of the profound transformation that can arise from adversity. Allow yourself to redefine your priorities, deepen your empathy, and cultivate a life filled with purpose and meaning.

The road ahead may be winding, but the lessons and wisdom you've gained will guide you every step of the way. Trust in your strength, lean into your support network, and never lose sight of the incredible person you've become through this journey. Healing and thriving are not only possible – they are your birthright.

CONCLUSION

As we reach the end of this comprehensive guide, it's important to reflect on the transformative journey you've undertaken. From the depths of narcissistic abuse, you've emerged as a warrior, a survivor, and a beacon of resilience. The path to healing has been arduous, but the wisdom and strength you've gained along the way are invaluable gifts that will serve you for a lifetime.

Summary of Key Points

Throughout this book, we've explored the multifaceted aspects of healing from narcissistic abuse, a journey that encompasses understanding the tactics of narcissists, unpacking the trauma, and ultimately reclaiming your power and thriving in the aftermath. Let's revisit some of the key points that have paved the way for your healing and growth:

1.   Understanding Narcissistic Abuse

We began by shedding light on the insidious nature of narcissistic abuse, a form of emotional manipulation that can leave deep psychological scars. We delved into the characteristics of narcissistic personality disorder, the common tactics employed by narcissists, and the devastating impact of emotional abuse on the mind, body, and spirit.

2.   Leaving the Abusive Situation

Recognizing the need to leave an abusive situation is a crucial first step, but it's often the most challenging. We explored strategies for safety planning, accessing support resources, and coping with the fears, doubts, and setbacks that inevitably arise during this process.

3.   Unpacking the Trauma

Narcissistic abuse can result in complex trauma, including PTSD and trauma bonding. We examined the role of professional support, such as therapists and support groups, in navigating triggers, flashbacks, and the intricate process of healing from emotional wounds.

4.   Rebuilding Self-Worth

At the core of healing lies the journey of rediscovering and reclaiming your inherent self-worth. We delved into techniques for challenging internalized criticism, fostering self-compassion, and rediscovering your authentic identity beyond the confines of abuse.

5.   Healthy Boundaries and Relationships

Establishing and enforcing healthy boundaries is paramount in your life after abuse. We explored strategies for setting limits, recognizing red flags in new relationships, and cultivating a supportive network that nurtures your growth and well-being.

6.   Personal Growth and Empowerment

Healing is not merely about surviving; it's about thriving. We explored ways to pursue your passions, goals, and a deeper sense of meaning, while developing resilience, emotional intelligence, and the courage to let go of the past and embrace forgiveness.

7.   Maintaining Healing and Wisdom

The journey of healing is not linear, and setbacks are natural. We delved into relapse prevention strategies, the importance of sharing your lessons with others, and the profound role of post-traumatic growth in shaping a life filled with purpose and wisdom.

INSPIRATIONAL MESSAGES OF HOPE

As you reflect on the lessons and insights gained throughout this book, it's important to remember that you are not alone in this journey. Countless survivors have walked this path before you, emerging not only healed but also empowered, resilient, and deeply connected to their inner strength.

Your story is one of resilience, perseverance, and ultimately, triumph over adversity. The challenges you've faced have forged a depth of character, self-awareness, and wisdom that will serve as a guiding light for the rest of your life.

Remember, healing is not a destination; it's a continuous process of growth, self-discovery, and embracing the beauty of your authentic self.

Each day presents an opportunity to recommit to your well-being, to honor the lessons you've learned, and to celebrate the remarkable person you've become.

As you move forward, carry these inspirational messages of hope in your heart:

1.   You are Stronger than You Know

The very fact that you've made it this far is a testament to your incredible strength and resilience. The obstacles you've overcome have revealed depths of courage and determination that may have been hidden before. Embrace this inner strength and let it guide you towards a future filled with possibility and empowerment.

2.   **Your Healing Journey is Unique**

While there may be commonalities in the experiences of survivors, your path to healing is uniquely yours. Honor your journey, celebrate your milestones, and trust the wisdom that emerges from your lived experiences. There is no one-size-fits-all approach; embrace the authenticity of your personal growth.

3.   You Deserve Happiness and Fulfillment

Narcissistic abuse can rob you of your sense of self-worth and the belief that you deserve happiness and fulfillment. But this is a lie perpetuated by the abuser. You are worthy of love, respect, and the pursuit of your dreams. Reclaim your power and unapologetically embrace the life you deserve.

4.   Your Scars are a Reminder of Your Resilience

The emotional scars left by narcissistic abuse are not signs of weakness or failure; they are badges of honor, reminders of the battles you've fought and the resilience you've cultivated. Wear these scars with pride, for they represent the depth of your strength and the incredible journey you've undertaken.

5.   You have the Power to Create Positive Change

Through your healing journey, you've gained invaluable wisdom and insights that can benefit others. Embrace the opportunity to advocate, educate, and inspire those who may still be trapped in the cycle of abuse. Your voice has the power to create positive change and shed light on this often-misunderstood form of trauma.

6.   Your Future is Filled with Possibility

While the past may hold painful memories, the future is a blank canvas waiting for you to paint your masterpiece. Embrace the limitless possibilities that lie ahead, and approach each day with a sense of wonder, curiosity, and the courage to explore new horizons.

7.   You are Worthy of Love and Belonging

Narcissistic abuse can shatter your sense of self-worth and leave you feeling unlovable. But this is a distortion perpetuated by the abuser. You are worthy of love, belonging, and authentic connections. Surround yourself with those who see your true value and celebrate the magnificence of your soul.

As you carry these messages of hope and inspiration with you, remember that your healing journey is a testament to your resilience, courage, and the indomitable spirit that resides within you. Embrace the wisdom you've gained, share your light with others, and continue to walk the path of self-discovery and personal growth.

RESOURCES FOR FURTHER SUPPORT

While this book has aimed to provide a comprehensive guide to healing and thriving after narcissistic abuse, the journey is a deeply personal one, and additional support may be necessary at various stages. Here are some valuable resources to help you continue your healing journey:

1.   **Therapy and Counseling**

Working with a licensed therapist or counselor who specializes in narcissistic abuse, trauma, and PTSD can be invaluable. They can provide personalized guidance, evidence-based techniques, and a safe space to process your experiences and emotions. Consider seeking out therapists who specialize in modalities such as EMDR, somatic therapy, or trauma-focused cognitive-behavioral therapy.

2.   **Support Groups**

Connecting with others who have experienced similar forms of abuse can provide a sense of validation, understanding, and community. Look for in-person or online support groups specifically focused on narcissistic abuse recovery. Sharing your story and hearing from others can foster a sense of hope and belonging.

3. Educational Resources

Continuing to educate yourself about narcissistic abuse, trauma recovery, and personal growth can deepen your understanding and provide new perspectives. Explore books, websites, podcasts, and online courses created by reputable experts and survivors in this field.

4. Self-Care and Wellness Practices

Prioritizing self-care and incorporating practices that nurture your physical, emotional, and spiritual well-being can significantly enhance your healing journey. Consider exploring mindfulness practices, yoga, art therapy, journaling, or engaging in activities that bring you joy and a sense of inner peace.

5.   Legal and Financial Assistance

For those who have experienced financial abuse or are navigating legal complexities related to their situation, seeking professional guidance from lawyers, financial advisors, or domestic violence organizations can provide invaluable support and resources.

6.   Crisis Hotlines and Emergency Services

If you are experiencing a mental health crisis or find yourself in an unsafe situation, do not hesitate to reach out for immediate assistance. Hotlines, such as the National Domestic Violence Hotline (1-800-799-SAFE) or the National Suicide Prevention Lifeline (1-800-273-TALK), can provide crisis intervention and connect you with local resources and emergency services.

Remember, healing is a journey, and seeking support is a sign of strength, not weakness. Embrace the resources available to you and surround yourself with a network of professionals, peers, and loved ones who can offer guidance, validation, and encouragement every step of the way.

As you embark on the next chapter of your life, filled with healing, hope, and empowerment, remember that your story is one of resilience, courage, and ultimately, triumph over adversity. The challenges you've faced have forged a depth of character, self-awareness, and wisdom that will serve as a guiding light for the rest of your life.

Embrace the lessons you've learned, celebrate the remarkable person you've become, and carry the hope of a future filled with possibility, authenticity, and joy. You have survived the darkest of storms, and now, the path ahead is illuminated by the radiance of your own inner strength.

With each step, you are rewriting the narrative of your life, shedding the shackles of abuse and emerging as a beacon of hope for others who may still be trapped in the cycle of manipulation and emotional turmoil. Your journey is a testament to the indomitable spirit of the human soul and the profound capacity for healing and growth that resides within us all.

As you move forward, may you walk with confidence, compassion, and a deep sense of gratitude for the lessons that have shaped you. Embrace the beauty of your authentic self, cherish the connections that nourish your soul, and fearlessly pursue the dreams and passions that set your heart ablaze.

Remember, you are a survivor, a warrior, and a force of nature. The world awaits your brilliance, your resilience, and the light you have to offer. So, step boldly into the future, knowing that you have the power to create the life you truly deserve – a life of healing, hope, and empowerment.

If you found this book helpful on your journey of healing from narcissistic abuse, I would be incredibly grateful if you could take a moment to leave a review on Amazon. Your honest feedback not only helps others find this resource as they navigate their own paths to recovery, but it also provides valuable insights for improving future editions.

Leaving a review is simple - just visit the book's page on Amazon, click on the "Customer Reviews" section, and share your thoughts. Every review makes a difference in raising awareness about this important topic and supporting fellow survivors.

Your words of encouragement or criticism can make a profound impact, providing guidance to those still trapped in the cycle of abuse or validating the experiences of those working towards healing. Together, we can create a community of support, hope, and empowerment for all affected by narcissistic abuse.

Thank you for being part of this journey. Your courage and resilience are an inspiration, and I am honored to have played a small role in your path towards reclaiming your life and thriving.